UNIVERSITY OF MINNESOTA

Ernest Hemingway

88

BY PHILIP YOUNG

UNIVERSITY OF MINNESOTA PRESS • MINNEAPOLIS

Printed in the United States of America at
the Jones Press, Inc., Minneapolis

Library of Congress Catalog Card Number: 59-63267

PUBLISHED IN GREAT BRITAIN, INDIA, AND PAKISTAN BY THE OXFORD
UNIVERSITY PRESS, LONDON, BOMBAY, AND KARACHI AND IN
CANADA BY THOMAS ALLEN, LTD., TORONTO

⤺ *Foreword*

Aᴍᴇʀɪᴄᴀɴ literature is one of the world's youngest literatures. In many ways it is an offshoot of English literature, but, as the editor of the London *Times Literary Supplement* said a few years ago, it has achieved its own independence and vigor. Especially in the years since World War II, both in the United States and in other countries, the interest in American writers has increased greatly.

The University of Minnesota Pamphlets on American Writers are designed to help satisfy this interest. The editors and advisers hope that students in various parts of the world will bring to these pamphlets the same sort of attention that serious students, in either hemisphere or in whatever zone, have traditionally brought to the various national literatures that have engaged their minds and have stimulated their imaginations. They also hope each pamphlet will provide a worthwhile critical summary (as well as a brief biographical sketch and bibliography) that will serve the needs of mature readers in all countries. Ideally, of course, each pamphlet should send the reader to the writer's own books, upon which he can pass his own critical judgments.

In the seventeenth and eighteenth centuries the United States produced only a small number of writers. In the nineteenth century the number increased greatly, and in the twentieth it has become almost a flood. In the opinion of the editors and advisers the authors being discussed in this series are those who have won, or seem to deserve, a place among the world's important writers.

William Van O'Connor, Allen Tate, and
Robert Penn Warren, ᴇᴅɪᴛᴏʀꜱ

ERNEST HEMINGWAY

PHILIP YOUNG is a professor of American literature at the Pennsylvania State University. His book-length study *Ernest Hemingway* was published by Rinehart in 1952. It was also published in England and has been translated into several foreign languages.

✓ *Ernest Hemingway*

THE first short story in Ernest Hemingway's first book of short stories — it was indeed his first significant book of any kind — is called "Indian Camp." It tells of a doctor named Adams and his son Nick, who go to a camp of Indians in northern Michigan where the doctor delivers a baby by Caesarian section, with a jack-knife and without anesthetic. The woman's invalid husband lies in a bunk above his screaming wife; Nick, a young boy, holds a basin for his father; a man and three women hold the mother down until the child is born. When it is over the doctor looks in the bunk above and discovers that the husband, who has listened to the screaming for two days, has cut his head nearly off with a razor.

A careful reading of this story will show that Hemingway is not primarily interested here in these shocking events. He is more interested in their effect on the little boy who witnessed them. As a matter of fact the events do not seem, at the time, to have any remarkable effect on the boy. But later on this same Nick Adams is a badly scarred and nervous young man, and in this story Hemingway is relating to us one of the many reasons why.

The author of this story is very probably America's most famous living writer of fiction. His style, his "hero" (that is to say the protagonists of many of his works, who so resemble each other that we have come to speak of them in the singular), his manner and attitudes are very widely recognized throughout the world. He is also quite possibly the most influential writer of

3

English prose in our century, for in nearly every country where his work is known it has been used: imitated, reworked, or assimilated. In addition Hemingway has a great reputation as a colorful human being, and for over a quarter of a century his every escapade has been duly reported in the press. But for a long time neither he nor his work was well understood. Neither is yet understood as well as it might be, and one of the chief reasons has been a failure to discern the center of Hemingway's interest in such a story as "Indian Camp," and to understand the book in which it appeared.

The book came out in 1925, and is called *In Our Time*. Very probably the author intended his title as a sardonic allusion to a phrase from the Church of England's Book of Common Prayer: "Give peace in our time, O Lord." At any rate the most striking thing about the volume is that there is no peace at all in the stories. The next most striking thing about them (long unremarked, since it was not clear that Nick is the central figure in the stories in which he appears) is that half of the stories are devoted to the spotty but careful development of a crucial character — a boy, then a young man — named Nick Adams. These stories are arranged in the chronological order of Nick's boyhood and young manhood, and are intimately related, one to another. Indeed in this aspect the book is almost a "novel," for some of the stories are incomprehensible if one does not see the point, and it is often subtle, of some earlier story.

There are six other stories about Nick in this volume. None of them is quite so violent as "Indian Camp," but all of them are in some way unpleasant or upsetting. In one, "The Doctor and the Doctor's Wife," Nick discovers that he is unsure about his father's courage and is completely dissatisfied with his mother's way of looking at things. Two others, "The End of Something" and "The Three-Day Blow," detail among other matters the

4

disturbing end of an adolescent love affair. In "The Battler" Nick is knocked off a moving freight train by a brakeman, and encounters a crazy ex-prizefighter who nearly beats him up, along with an extremely polite Negro hobo who in his own way is even more sinister. One should suspect that Nick is being exposed to more than may be entirely good for him.

Immediately following "The Battler" comes a little sketch, less than a page long, which serves to confirm this suspicion. It tells us that Nick is in World War I, that he has been wounded, and that he has made a "separate peace" with the enemy — is not fighting for his country, or any other, any more. It would be quite impossible to exaggerate the importance of this short scene in any understanding of Hemingway and his work. It will be duplicated at more length by another protagonist, named Frederic Henry, in *A Farewell to Arms*, and it will serve as a climax in the lives of all of Hemingway's heroes, in one way or another, for at least the next quarter-century.

The fact that Nick is seriously injured is significant in two important ways. First, the wound intensifies and epitomizes the wounds he has been getting as a boy growing up in the American Midwest. From here on the Hemingway hero will appear to us as a wounded man — wounded not only physically but, as soon becomes clear, psychologically as well. Second, the fact that Nick and his friend, also wounded, have made a "separate peace," are "Not patriots," marks the beginning of the long break with organized society as a whole that stays with Hemingway and his hero through several books to come, and into the late 1930's. Indeed the last story in this first volume, called "Big Two-Hearted River," is a kind of forecast of these things. It is obscure until one sees the point, and almost completely so; its author complained in 1950 that the tale was twenty-five years old and still had not been understood by anyone. But it is really a very simple

5

"story." It is a study of a young man who has been hurt in the war, who is all by himself on a fishing trip, escaping everyone. He is suffering from what used to be called "shell shock"; he is trying desperately to keep from going out of his mind.

In his next two collections of short stories, *Men without Women* (1927) and *Winner Take Nothing* (1933), Hemingway included several more stories about Nick Adams. They do not change anything, but they fill in some of the gaps in his sketchy career. In one, an eternally reprinted tale called "The Killers," he is exposed to a sickening situation in which a man refuses to run any more from some gangsters who are clearly going to murder him. In another, "The Light of the World," he is somewhat prematurely introduced into the seamy realms of prostitution and homosexuality. In a third, "Fathers and Sons," he is deeply troubled by thoughts of his father's death. (At the time we cannot know exactly why, and do not know until many years later when the hero, now under the name of Robert Jordan, in *For Whom the Bell Tolls,* returns to this situation and explains; Doctor Adams committed suicide.) And in a fourth, "A Way You'll Never Be," Nick meets the fate he was trying desperately to avoid in "Big Two-Hearted River" and, as a direct result of his war experiences, goes entirely out of his mind.

Further gaps in the picture we should have of Nick are filled by several stories Hemingway wrote in the first person. It is abundantly clear that the narrator of them is Nick, and in one of the tales, a war story called "Now I Lay Me," he is called by that name. This one is a story about insomnia, which Nick suffered for a long time following his wounding; he cannot sleep "for thinking," and several things that occupy his mind while he lies awake relate closely to scenes and events in stories already mentioned. "In Another Country" extends the range of Hemingway's essential interest from Nick to another individual casu-

6

alty of the war, and thus points toward *The Sun Also Rises,* where a whole "lost generation" has been damaged in the same disaster. A further development occurs in "An Alpine Idyll," which returns us to a postwar skiing trip Nick took in a tale called "Cross Country Snow"; here the interest focuses on the responses of Nick and others to a particularly shocking situation, as it did in the more famous "Killers." But whereas in the earlier story Nick was so upset by the thought of the man who was passively waiting to be murdered that he wanted to get clean out of the town where the violence impended, healthy tissue is now growing over his wounds, and the point of the story lies in the development of his defenses.

By now it is perfectly clear what kind of boy, then man, this Adams is. He is certainly not the simple primitive he is often mistaken for. He is honest, virile, but — clearest of all — very sensitive. He is an outdoor male, and he has a lot of nerve, but he is also very nervous. It is important to understand this Nick, for soon, under other names in other books, he is going to be known half the world over as the "Hemingway hero": every single one of these men has had, or has had the exact equivalent of, Nick's childhood, adolescence, and young manhood. This man will die a thousand times before his death, and although he will learn how to live with some of his troubles, and how to overcome others, he will never completely recover from his wounds as long as Hemingway lives and records his adventures.

Now it is also clear that something was needed to bind these wounds, and there is in Hemingway a consistent character who performs that function. This figure is not Hemingway himself in disguise (which to some hard-to-measure extent the Hemingway hero is). Indeed he is to be sharply distinguished from the hero, for he comes to balance the hero's deficiencies, to correct his stance. We generally, though unfelicitously, call this man the

7

"code hero" — this because he represents a code according to which the hero, if he could attain it, would be able to live properly in the world of violence, disorder, and misery to which he has been introduced and which he inhabits. The code hero, then, offers up and exemplifies certain principles of honor, courage, and endurance which in a life of tension and pain make a man a man, as we say, and enable him to conduct himself well in the losing battle that is life. He shows, in the author's famous phrase for it, "grace under pressure."

This man also makes his first appearance in the short stories. He is Jack, the prizefighter of "Fifty Grand," who through a superhuman effort manages to lose the fight he has promised to lose. He is Manuel, "The Undefeated" bullfighter who, old and wounded, simply will not give up when he is beaten. He is Wilson, the British hunting guide of "The Short Happy Life of Francis Macomber," who teaches his employer the shooting standards that make him, for a brief period preceding his death, a happy man. And, to distinguish him most clearly from the Hemingway hero, he is Cayetano, the gambler of "The Gambler, the Nun and the Radio," who with two bullets in his stomach will not show a single sign of suffering, while the generic Nick, here called Mr. Frazer, is shamed to suffer less but visibly. The finest and best known of these code heroes appears, however, in Hemingway's most recent novel. He is old Santiago of *The Old Man and the Sea.* The chief point about him is that he behaves perfectly — honorably, with great courage and endurance — while losing to the sharks the giant fish he has caught. This, to epitomize the message the code hero always brings, is life: you lose, of course; what counts is how you conduct yourself while you are being destroyed.

The three matters already introduced — the wound, the break from society, the code (and a working adjustment of these things)

8

— are the subjects of all of Hemingway's significant work outside as well as inside the short stories. This work comes to ten book-length pieces: six novels, a burlesque, a book on big-game hunting, one on bullfighting, and a play. The pattern already set up will, it is hoped, help to place these works and to clarify their meanings.

It will not help much with the first of them, however, for this is an anomaly: the burlesque, a "satirical novel," *The Torrents of Spring*. It appeared in 1926, and is a parody of Sherwood Anderson's novels in general, and of his *Dark Laughter* (1925) in particular. It is a moderately amusing performance, especially if one will first take the trouble to read or reread the specific object of attack; there were ridiculous elements even in Anderson's "better" novels, and Hemingway goes unerringly to them. But this book, dashed off in a great hurry, has never had as many readers as Hemingway's other books, and it has no relation to anything else he has written — except that in it he was declaring himself free of certain egregious weaknesses in a man who had at one time influenced him. It is said that he was also breaking his contract with his publishers, Boni and Liveright, who would feel that they must reject this satire on one of their leading writers; thus Hemingway would be free to take his work to Scribner's, whom he much preferred.

It is very doubtful that Hemingway intended his book primarily as a means whereby he might change publishers. But Liveright did reject it, Scribner's did bring it out, and thus Scribner's have been able to publish the rest of his work. Nor did they have to wait long to prove the wisdom of their acceptance of Hemingway, for his first true novel, *The Sun Also Rises*, came into their hands the same year. This book in time became a best seller and made its author's reputation. *The Sun Also Rises* reintroduces us to the hero, here called Jake Barnes. His wound, again with both literal and symbolic meanings, is transferred from the spine (where Nick

9

was hit) to the genitals: Jake was, to speak loosely, emasculated in the war. His wound, then, has undergone a significant transformation, but he is still the hero, still the man who cannot sleep when his head starts to work, and who cries in the night. He has also parted with society and the usual middle-class ways; he lives in Paris with an international group of expatriates, a dissolute collection of amusing but aimless people — all of them, in one way or another, blown out of the paths of ordinary life by the war. This was, as Gertrude Stein had remarked to Hemingway, the "lost generation," and in this book Hemingway made it famous.

Although it is not highly developed yet, Jake and the few people he likes have a code. There are certain things that are "done," and many that are "not done," and one of the characters distinguishes people as belonging or not belonging according to whether they understand or not. The whole trouble with Robert Cohn, a writer, for instance, is that he does not understand, and he is sharply juxtaposed to a young bullfighter named Romero (an early code hero) who, in the way he conducts himself both personally and professionally, does understand.

The action of the novel is taken up with drinking, fishing, and going to the bullfights, as well as with the promiscuous affairs of a young lady named Brett Ashley. Brett is in love with Jake, and he with her, but since he is wounded as he is there is not much they can do about it. Brett, although engaged to a man who like herself and Jake is a casualty of the war, passes from Cohn to Romero and then — because she has principles too — she leaves him and in the end is back, hopelessly, with Jake. Nothing leads anywhere in the book, and that is perhaps the real point of it. The action comes full circle — imitates, that is, the sun of the title, which also rises, only to hasten to the place where it arose (the title is, of course, a quotation from Ecclesiastes). For the most part the novel is a delightful one. The style is fresh and sparkling,

10

the dialogue is fun to read, and the book is beautifully and mean-
ingfully constructed. But its message is that for these people at
least (and one gets the distinct impression that other people do
not matter very much), life is futile.

It happens that this is not precisely the message Hemingway intended to give. He has said that he regarded the line "you are all
a lost generation," which he used as an epigraph, as a piece of
"splendid bombast," and that he included the passage from Ecclesiastes, also quoted as an epigraph, to correct the remark attrib-
uted to Miss Stein. As far as he was concerned, he wrote his editor
Maxwell Perkins, the point of his novel is, as the Biblical lines
say in part, that "the earth abideth forever."

To be sure, some support for these contentions can be found in
the novel itself. Not quite all the characters are "lost" — Romero
is not — and the beauty of the eternal earth is now and again richly invoked. But most of the characters do seem lost indeed, a great
deal of the time, and few readers have taken the passage from Ecclesiastes as Hemingway did. The strongest feeling in it is not that
the earth abides forever, but that all motion is endless, circular,
and unavailing; and for all who know what the Preacher said, the
echo of "Vanity of vanities; all is vanity" is nearly as strong. For
once Hemingway's purpose and accomplishment are here two
things, but the result is nonetheless impressive, and *The Sun Also
Rises* remains one of the two best novels he has written.

The other is his next book, *A Farewell to Arms* (1929), and one
thing it does is to explain how the characters of *The Sun Also
Rises*, and the hero particularly, got the way they are. In the
course of the novel Lt. Frederic Henry is wounded in the war as
was Nick Adams (although now the most serious of his injuries is
to his knee, which is where Hemingway himself was hardest hit).
Henry shows clearly the results of this misfortune; again he cannot sleep at night unless he stops thinking; again, when he does

sleep he has nightmares. While recuperating in Milan, he falls in love with an English nurse, but when he is returned to the front he is forced to desert the army in which he has been fighting in order to save his life. He escapes to Switzerland with the nurse, a compliant young woman named Catherine Barkley who is now pregnant with his child, and there she dies in childbirth. Henry is left, at the end, with nothing. A man is trapped, Hemingway seems to be saying. He is trapped biologically and he is trapped socially; either way it can only end badly, and there are no other ways.

Once again this is a beautifully written book. The prose is hard and clean, the people come to life instantly and ring true. The novel is built with scrupulous care. A short introductory scene at the very start presents an ominous conjunction of images — of rain, pregnancy, and death — which set the mood for, and prefigure, all that is to follow. Then the action is tied into a perfect and permanent knot by the skill with which the two themes are brought together. As the intentionally ambiguous title suggests, the two themes are of course love and war. (They are developments, incidentally, from two early fragments: the sketch, "Chapter VI," in which Nick was wounded, and the "love story," called "A Very Short Story," that immediately followed it in *In Our Time*.)

Despite the frequency of their appearance in the same books, love and war are — to judge from the frequency with which writers fail to wed them — an unlikely mixture. But in this novel their courses run exactly, though subtly, parallel, so that in the end we feel we have read one story, not two. In his affair with the war Henry goes through six phases: from desultory participation to serious action and a wound, and then through his recuperation in Milan to a retreat which leads to his desertion. Carefully interwoven with all this is his relationship with Catherine, which undergoes six precisely corresponding stages: from a trifling sexual affair to actual love and her conception, and then through her confinement in the Alps to a trip to the hospital which leads to her death. By the time the last farewell is taken, the stories are as one in the point, lest there be any sentimental doubt about it, that life, both personal and social, is a struggle in which the Loser Takes Nothing, either.

But like all of Hemingway's better books this one is bigger than any short account of it can indicate. For one thing there is the stature of Frederic Henry, and it is never more clear than here that he is the Hemingway "hero" in more senses than are suggested by the term "protagonist." Henry stands for many men; he stands for the experience of his country: in his evolution from complicity in the war to bitterness to escape, the whole of America could read its recent history in a crucial period, Wilson to Harding. When he expressed his disillusionment with the ideals the war claimed to promote, and jumped in a river and deserted, Henry's action epitomized the contemporary feeling of a whole nation. Not that the book is without positive values, however — as is often alleged, and as Robert Penn Warren, for one, has disproved. Henry progresses from the messiness represented by the brothel to the order that is love; he distinguishes sharply between the disciplined and competent people he has to do with and the disorderly and incompetent ones: the moral value of these virtues is not incidental to the action but a foundation on which the book is built. Despite such foundations, however, the final effect of this mixture of pessimism and ideals is one of tragedy and despair.

The connection between Hemingway and his hero has always been intimate, and in view of the pessimism of these last two books it is perhaps not surprising that his next two books, which were works of nonfiction, find the hero — Hemingway himself, now, without disguise — pretty much at the end of his rope, and in complete escape from the society he had renounced in *A Farewell to Arms*. The books are *Death in the Afternoon* (1932) and *Green Hills of Africa* (1935). Neither of them is of primary importance. The first is a book about bullfighting, one of a surprising number of subjects in which the author is learned; the second is a book on big-game hunting, about which he also knows a great deal. But the books are really about death — the death of bulls, bullfighters, horses, and big game; death is a subject which by his own admission has obsessed Hemingway for a long time. Both books are also a little hysterical, as if written under great nervous tension. To be sure the bullfighter is a good example of the man with the code. As he acts out his role as high priest of a ceremonial in which men pit themselves against violent death, and, with a behavior that formalizes the code, administers what men seek to avoid, he is the very personification of "grace under pressure." And both volumes contain long passages — on writing, Spain, Africa, and other subjects — that are well worth reading. But more clearly than anything else the books present the picture of a man who has, since that separate peace, cut himself so completely off from the roots that nourish that he is starving. The feeling is strong that he will have to find new roots, or re-establish old ones, if he is going to write any more good novels.

This process was not a painless one, and Hemingway's next book, *To Have and Have Not* (1937), amply betrays that fact. This is a novel, though not a good one — at least not for this novelist. But it is one in which its author clearly shows that he has learned something that will become very important to him before he is done writing. As often before, and later too, it is the code hero, piratically named Harry Morgan, who teaches the lesson. The novel tells the story of this man who is forced, since he cannot support his wife and children through honest work, to go his own way: he becomes an outlaw who smuggles rum and people into the United States from Cuba. In the end he is killed, but before he dies he has learned the lesson that Hemingway himself must recently have learned: alone, a man has no chance.

It is regrettable that this pronouncement, articulating a death-bed conversion, does not grow with any sense of inevitability out of the action of the book. A contrast between the Haves and the Have Nots of the story is meant to be structure and support for the novel and its message, but the whole affair is unconvincing. The superiority of the Nots is apparently based on the superiority of the sex life of the Morgans, on some savage disgust aimed at a successful writer in the book, and on some callow explanations of how the Haves got their money. Just how all these things lead to Harry's final pronouncement is Hemingway's business, and it is not skillfully transacted.

But the novel itself is of minor significance. What it represents in Hemingway is important. Here is the end of the long exile that began with Nick Adams' separate peace, the end of Hemingway's ideological separation from the world: a man has no chance alone. As a matter of fact, by 1937, the year of this novel, Hemingway had come close to embracing the society he had deserted some twenty years before, and was back in another "war for democracy."

More than any other single thing, it seems to have been the civil war in Spain that returned Hemingway to the world of other people. He was informally involved in that war, on the Loyalist side, and his next full-length work was a play, called *The Fifth Column* (1938), which praises the fighters with whom he was associated and declares his faith in their cause. The play is distinguished by some excellent talk, and marred by a kind of cops-and-robbers action. The Hemingway hero, now called simply Philip, is immediately recognizable. He is still afflicted with his memories, and with insomnia and horrors in the night. A kind of Scarlet Pimpernel

15

dressed as an American reporter, Philip appears to be a charming but dissolute wastrel, a newsman who never files any stories. But actually, and unknown to his mistress, Dorothy, he is up to his neck in the Loyalist fight. The most striking thing about him, however, is the distance he has come from the hero, so like him in every other way, who decided in *A Farewell to Arms* that such faiths and causes were "obscene."

But it is almost no distance at all from the notion that a man has no chance alone to the thought that "No man is an *Iland*, intire of itself. . . ." These words, from a devotion by John Donne, are part of an epigraph to Hemingway's next novel, whose title, *For Whom the Bell Tolls* (1940), comes from the same source. The bell referred to is a funeral bell: "And therefore never send to know for whom the *bell* tolls; It tolls for *thee*."

/ This time the novel is true to its controlling concept. It deals with three days in the life of the Hemingway hero, now named Robert Jordan, who is fighting as an American volunteer in the Spanish civil war. He is sent to join a guerrilla band in the mountains near Segovia to blow up a strategic bridge, thus facilitating a Loyalist advance. He spends three days and nights in the guerrillas' cave, while he awaits what he expects will be his own destruction, and he falls in love with Maria, the daughter of a Republican mayor who has been murdered — as she herself has been raped — by the Falangists. Jordan believes the attack will fail, but the generals will not cancel it until it is too late. He successfully destroys the bridge, is wounded in the retreat, and is left to die. But he has come to see the wisdom of such a sacrifice, and the book ends without bitterness.

This is not a flawless novel. For one thing the love story, if not sentimental, is at any rate idealized and very romantic; for another, there are a good many passages in which Jordan appears more to be struggling for the faith on which he acts than to have

achieved it. The hero is still the wounded man, and new incidents
from his past are supplied to explain why this is so; two of the
characters remark pointedly that he was too young to experience
the things he tells them of having experienced. But Jordan has
learned a lot, since the old days, about how to live and function
with his wounds, and he behaves well. He dies, but he has done
his job, and the manner of his dying convinced many readers of
what his thinking had failed to do: that life is worth living and
that there are causes worth dying for.

The skill with which this novel was for the most part written
demonstrated that Hemingway's talent was once again intact and
formidable. None of his books had evoked more richly the life of
the senses, had shown a surer sense of plotting, or provided more
fully living secondary characters, or livelier dialogue. But following this success (this was the most successful of all his books so
far as sales are concerned), he lapsed into a silence that lasted a
whole decade — chiefly because of nonliterary activities in connection with World War II. And when he broke this silence in 1950
with his next book, a novel called *Across the River and into the
Trees,* the death of his once-great talent was very widely advertised
by the critics and reviewers.

To be sure, this is a poor performance. It is the story of a peacetime army colonel (but almost an exact self-portrait) who comes
on leave to Venice to go duck-shooting, to see his very young girl
friend, and to die, all of which he does. The colonel is the hero
again, this time called Richard Cantwell, and he has all the old
scars, particularly the specific ones he received as Frederic Henry
in *A Farewell to Arms.* Again there is the "Hemingway heroine,"
a title that designates the British nurse, Catherine, of that novel,
and the Spanish girl Maria of *For Whom the Bell Tolls,* and now
the young Italian countess Renata of this novel. (They are all
pretty much the same girl, though for some reason their national-

ity keeps changing, as the hero's never does, and they grow young-
er as the hero ages.) There are also many signs of the "code." But
the code in this book has become a sort of joke; the hero has become a good deal of a bore, and the heroine has become a wispy
dream. The distance that Hemingway once maintained between
himself and his protagonist has disappeared, to leave us with a
self-indulgent chronicling of the author's every opinion; he acts
as though he were being interviewed. The novel reads like a parody of the earlier works.

But there is one interesting thing about it. Exactly one hundred
years before the appearance of this novel Nathaniel Hawthorne
published *The Scarlet Letter*, in which he wrote: "There is a fa-
tality, a feeling so irresistible and inevitable that it has the force
of doom, which almost invariably compels human beings to linger
around and haunt, ghostlike, the spot where some great and
marked event has given the color to their lifetime; and still the
more irresistibly, the darker the tinge that saddens it." From Hawthorne himself and Poe, from Hawthorne's Hester Prynne and
Melville's Ahab right down to J. D. Salinger's "Zooey," who is un-
willing to leave New York ("I've been *run over* here — twice, and
on the same damn *street*") — no one in the history of American
letters has demonstrated Hawthorne's insight with as much force
and clarity as have Hemingway and his hero. And nowhere in
Hemingway is the demonstration more clear than in *Across the
River and into the Trees*, for it is here that Colonel Cantwell
makes a sort of pilgrimage to the place where he — and where
Nick Adams, and Frederic Henry (and Hemingway himself) —
was first wounded. He takes instruments, and locates by survey the
exact place on the ground where he had been struck. Then, in
an act of piercing, dazzling identification, he builds a very personal sort of monument to the spot, acknowledges and confronts
the great, marked event that colored his lifetime — and Heming-

18

way's writing-time — and comes to the end of his journey (or the
end so far), not at the place where he first lived, but where first
he died.

The critics who professed to see in this book the death of
Hemingway's talent, as well as of his hero, happily proved to be
mistaken, for they were forced almost unanimously to accept his
next book, called *The Old Man and the Sea,* as a triumph. This
very short novel, which some insist on calling rather a long short
story (and it has for some time been rumored to be part of a
longer work-in-progress), concerns an old Cuban fisherman. After
eighty-four days without a fish Santiago ventures far out to sea
alone, and hooks a giant marlin in the Gulf Stream. For two days
and two nights the old man holds on while he is towed farther
out to sea; finally he brings the fish alongside, harpoons it, and
lashes it to his skiff. Almost at once the sharks begin to take his
prize away from him. He kills them until he has only his broken
tiller to fight with. Then they eat all but the skeleton, and he
tows that home, half dead with exhaustion, and makes his way
to bed to sleep and dream of other days.

The only thing that keeps *The Old Man and the Sea* from
greatness is the sense one has that the author is imitating instead
of creating the style that made him famous. But this reservation
is almost made up for by the book's abundance of meaning. As
always the code hero, here Santiago, comes with a message, and
it is essentially that while a man may grow old, and be wholly
down on his luck, he can still dare, stick to the rules, persist when
he is licked, and thus by the manner of his losing win his victory.
On another level the story can be read as an allegory entirely personal to its author, as an account of his own struggle, his determi-
nation, and his literary vicissitudes. Like Hemingway, Santiago is
a master who sets out his lines with more care and precision than
his competitors, but he has not had any luck in a long time. Once

he was very strong, the champion, yet his whole reputation is imperiled now, and he is growing old. Still he feels that he has strength enough; he knows the tricks of his trade; he is resolute, and he is still out for the really big success. It means nothing that he has proved his strength before; he has got to prove it again, and he does. After he has caught his prize the sharks come and take it all away from him, as they will always try to do. But he caught it, he fought it well, he did all he could and it was a lot, and at the end he is happy.

To take the broadest view, however, the novel is a representation of life as a struggle against unconquerable natural forces in which a kind of victory is possible. It is an epic metaphor for life, a contest in which even the problem of right and wrong seems paltry before the great thing that is the struggle. It is also something like Greek tragedy, in that as the hero falls and fails, the audience may get a memorable glimpse of what stature a man may have. And it is Christian tragedy as well, especially in the several marked allusions to Christian symbolism, particularly of the crucifixion — a development in Hemingway's novels that begins, apparently without much importance, in the early ones, gathers strength in *Across the River and into the Trees,* and comes to a kind of climax in this book.

Although the view of life in this novel had a long evolution from the days of total despair, it represents nonetheless an extraordinary change in its author. A reverence for life's struggle, and for mankind, seems to have descended on Hemingway like the gift of grace on the religious. The knowledge that a simple man is capable of the decency, dignity, and even heroism that Santiago possesses, and that his battle can be seen in heroic terms, is itself, technical considerations for the moment aside, perhaps the greatest victory that Hemingway has won. Very likely this is the sort of thing he had in mind when he remarked to someone, shortly after finishing the book, that he had got, finally, what he had been working for all of his life.

Hemingway is reported to have a good deal of unpublished material ready, or near-ready, for the printer, but he has brought out nothing since *The Old Man and the Sea* — save only two short stories, which appeared in the Centennial Issue of the *Atlantic Monthly* (November 1957) and are not, regrettably, of special note. At least a part of the probable reason for this silence is not far to seek: taxes. Hemingway is in that not altogether unenviable position where a substantial part of the profit from new work goes to the government. If, however, he leaves, say, a couple of novels and some stories behind him (the profits from a single short story, "The Snows of Kilimanjaro," must by now be approaching $200,000), then his present wife, his three sons, and his grandchildren should be fairly well off.

Hemingway the man is of considerable interest, and his life has been colorful. His story, at crucial points, is not unlike the story of his hero. He was born Ernest Miller Hemingway in an intensely middle-class suburb of Chicago called Oak Park, Illinois, on July 21, 1899. His father was a doctor, devoted to hunting and fishing; his mother was a religious and musical woman, and a struggle over which direction the boy should take appears to have been won by the former. The parts of his childhood that seem to have stayed most deeply with Hemingway were spent up in Michigan on vacations, and are reflected in several of the stories about young Nick Adams.

As a boy Hemingway learned to box (permanently damaging an eye in the process) and he played high-school football. He was not much pleased with the latter activity, however, partly because he was already more interested in writing. Working for his English classes and the school paper, he composed light verse; wrote a good many columns in imitation of Ring Lardner (a practice at which he became very adept), and tried his hand at some short stories. Although it looked for many years as though he was cut out to be a humorist, he also turned his hand to more serious fiction, and this is really the most impressive part of his juvenilia; already he was choosing to write about northern Michigan, and many of the features of his later style — especially some of the earmarks of his famous dialogue — are discernible in this early prose.

About half-seriously, doubtless, Hemingway remarked a few years ago that the best training for a writer is an unhappy boyhood. He himself, however, appears to have been reasonably happy a good part of the time. But he seems also to have been on occasion deeply dissatisfied with his homelife and with Oak Park. Twice he was a runaway, and no sooner did he graduate from high school than he was off for Kansas City, never really to return home. If it had not been for parental objections that he was too young (seventeen), and if not for his bad eye, he would have gone much farther away, for he was desperately eager to get into the war. Repeatedly rejected by the army, he went instead to the Kansas City *Star,* then one of the country's best newspapers, lied about his age (which accounts for the fact that his birth date is almost invariably given as 1898), and partly on the strength of his high-school newspaper experience landed a job as a reporter. Here he was known for his energy and eagerness, and for the fact that, in the line of duty, he always wanted to ride the ambulances. Finally able to get into the war as an honorary lieutenant in the Red Cross, he went overseas, in a state of very great excitement, as an ambulance driver. He was severely wounded, while passing out chocolate to the troops in Italy, at Fossalta di Piave, on July 8, 1918, and was decorated by the Italians for subsequent heroism. A dozen operations were performed on his knee, and after his recuperation in Milan he was with the Italian infantry until the Armistice.

After the war, "literally shot to pieces," according to a friend, he returned to the United States, his riddled uniform with him. Heading for northern Michigan again, he spent a time reading, writing, and fishing. Then he worked for a while in Canada for the Toronto *Star*, moved temporarily to Chicago, found himself unhappy with America, married, and took off for Paris as a foreign correspondent, employed again by the Toronto *Star*. He served in this role for some time, and then settled down in Paris to become once and for all, under the guidance of Gertrude Stein and others, a writer. Though it brought little in the way of money, his work soon began to attract attention, and *The Sun Also Rises* made him famous while he was still in his twenties. Since that time he has had no serious extended financial troubles, and with both critics and the general public has commanded a very wide following.

From other standpoints, Hemingway's story has been one of mixed success and failure. His first three marriages — to Hadley Richardson, the mother of his first son, to Pauline Pfeiffer, the mother of his second two boys, and to Martha Gellhorn, the novelist — all ended in divorce. (His present wife is the former Mary Welsh of Minnesota — all the other wives came from St. Louis — whom he met in England in 1944.) For a long time, the whole span of the thirties during which he lived mostly in Key West, Florida, his work did more to advance his reputation as sportsman and athlete than as a writer of memorable fiction. During the forties his nonliterary activities were even more spectacular, and though he published only one book in this period he was very much alive. There is subject matter for several romantic novels in his World War II adventures alone.

In 1942 he volunteered himself and his fishing boat, the *Pilar*, for various projects to the Navy, was accepted, and for two years cruised off the coast of Cuba with a somewhat suicidal plan for the destruction of U-boats in the area. In 1944 he was in England, and as an accredited correspondent went on several missions with the RAF. Shortly before the invasion of France he was in an auto wreck which necessitated the taking of fifty-seven stitches in his head. But he pulled the stitches out on D-Day, and after the break-through in Normandy attached himself to the division of his choice, the Fourth of the First Army, with which he saw considerable action at Schnee Eifel, in Luxembourg, and in the disaster at Hürtgen Forest. At one point in a battle, according to the commanding officer of the division ("I always keep a pin in the map for old Ernie Hemingway"), he was sixty miles in front of anything else in the First Army. Ostensibly a correspondent he was by now running his own small, informal, but effective army — motorized, equipped with "every imaginable" German and American weapon, and nearly weighed down with bottles and explosives. The history books have it that the French liberated their own capital from the Germans, and so they did, but the fact remains that Hemingway and his company of irregulars were engaged in a skirmish at the Arc de Triomphe when Leclerc's army was at the south bank of the Seine. The writer and his troops were soon billeted at the Ritz, which they had exclusively liberated.

The Heroic Hemingway and the Public Hemingway have produced somehow a Legendary Hemingway, an imaginary person who departs from the actual one at some point that is next to impossible to define. There is something about him that excites strange enthusiasms and even stranger antipathies. A good deal of what we think we know about him carries an air of having been gone over by a press agent. But some facts can be verified. In addition to the ones already given, it can be stated that Hem-

24

ingway lives on a "farm" called Finca Vigia on a hilltop at San Francisco de Paula, nine miles outside Havana; that he is generous, extremely perceptive about people, deeply and widely read as a student of literature, a bit of a linguist, and an expert in navigation, military history, and tactics. It is perhaps also relevant to note that he is in some private, unorthodox way a convert to Roman Catholicism. In view of the personal difficulties following his wounding in World War I, it is certainly relevant to record the fact that through a rigorous exercise of an impressive will, he has overcome his fears; professional soldiers in World War II have testified that he seemed to them the bravest man they had ever seen.

He is a gifted, strong personality, and at times eccentric. In *Across the River and into the Trees* Cantwell's driver speculates that some of the colonel's eccentricities are the result of his having been so often injured. Although this diagnosis may seem both offhand and indirect, one of the consequences of Hemingway's physical adventures is that he, like Cantwell, physically retains the record of about as many blows as a man may take and live. Understandably he does not wish to go down in history for this fact. But there seems little or no danger of that, and a list of his major injuries is certainly impressive and possibly significant. His skull has been fractured at least once; he has sustained at least a dozen brain concussions, several of them serious ones; he has been in three serious automobile accidents; and a few years ago in the African jungle he was in two airplane accidents in the space of two days, during which time he suffered severe internal injuries, "jammed" his spine, and received a concussion so violent that his eyesight was impaired for some time. (It was on this occasion that quite a few newspapers printed obituaries, which he read, after his recovery, with great pleasure; the notices were favorable.) In warfare alone he has been shot through nine parts of the body, and has sustained six head wounds. When he was blown up in Italy at the age of eighteen, and was left, for a time, for dead, the doctors removed all of the 237 steel fragments which had penetrated him that they could get at.

Some amount of such gossip is relevant to any discussion of Hemingway's work if only because it confirms and informs the picture of him which the work has given us. Our view of that work is in turn informed and confirmed by modern psychology, which offers an account of how many of the things to be found in Hemingway come to be there. This is no place to go into the niceties and vagaries of contemporary psychoanalytic theory, much of it post-Freudian, but it is perhaps not out of place to remark that such theory does give an explanation of the pre-occupations Hemingway's books and life reflect. His hero's night-mares and insomnia (attendant on his first serious wounding), his preoccupation with death, and with the scene of what was nearly his own premature end, his devotion to hunting and fishing, his intellectual limitations — all these things and several others may be accounted for in psychoanalytic terms. They used to be called symptoms of "shell shock"; now it is called "traumatic neurosis." The name matters very little. The point is that our understanding of Hemingway has medical backing, if such is desired. The point is further that his work has so faithfully and accurately docu-mented how this kind of illness conducts itself that it in turn lends considerable credence to the medical theory.

There should be no inference here that this point in any way detracts from what Hemingway has accomplished. Emphatically the contrary. "The world breaks everyone and afterward many are strong at the broken places," he remarked in A Farewell to Arms. His own career has been an extraordinary illustration of that notion. He has developed his strength, personal and esthetic, into a formidable thing, and the experience of a great many

26

people could be offered to show that the more one knows of the man and what he has accomplished, the more admiration one is likely to have for him.

But primary attention should go of course to Hemingway the writer, not the man — and still less the case-history — and there is little doubt that his technical achievement has been great. Indeed in the view of many people it is his simple, fresh, and clean prose style that is his true claim to renown and permanence. Those responsible for bestowing the Nobel Prize for Literature seemed to reflect this view, for in 1954 when he was awarded it they cited "his powerful style-forming mastery of the art of modern narration. . . ."

It is of course not true, as has been alleged, that this style sprang from nowhere. Actually it had a long evolution, which may be said to have begun when Mark Twain wrote the first paragraph of his *Adventures of Huckleberry Finn* (1884). What Twain was trying to do in this novel is very clear. He was trying to write as an American boy might speak — write, that is, not a "literary" English style, but a natural spoken English. Or rather a natural spoken American, for Twain was the first man to "write American," at least to do it really well. He found a freshness and a poetry in that speech which have not diminished one particle with the passing of the years. It is far too much to say, as Hemingway himself has said, that "all modern American literature" comes from that one book, but the book does indeed represent the true beginning of a widespread contemporary American style.

Other writers came between Twain and Hemingway in this evolution. It would be possible to draw up an extraordinary list of parallels between the lives and personalities of Hemingway and an intervening writer: Stephen Crane. Both men began their careers very young as reporters, then foreign correspondents. Both journeyed widely to wars. Each was profoundly shocked by the death of his father; each childhood was marred by the experience of violence; each man found in warfare an absorbing formalization of violence and an essential metaphor for life. Each tested himself against violence and in the end was cited for courage — and so on and on. Perhaps all this helps to account for the fact that a great many of the characteristics of Hemingway's prose — its intensity, its terse, unliterary tone, and many of the features of the dialogue, for instances — can be found first, when he is at his best, in Crane. (This is a debt which Hemingway has also, obliquely, acknowledged.)

Any effort to write a simple, spare, concise, and yet repetitive prose — clean, free of cliché and "artful" synonyms and all but the smallest and simplest of words — could and did benefit as well from the efforts of Gertrude Stein. In addition, Hemingway's early stories show a debt to Sherwood Anderson, and a good many other writers seem also to have had at least a small hand in the forming of him. The names F. Scott Fitzgerald, Ezra Pound, Ring Lardner, Joseph Conrad, Ford Madox Ford, and Ivan Turgenev should appear, among others, on any list that pretended to be complete.

Almost all writers show their chief debts in their earliest work. In Hemingway's case, however, the situation is complicated by the fact that eighteen of his earliest stories, and the first draft of a first novel — the better part of his production for four years — were in a suitcase that was stolen from his first wife on a train to Lausanne. Thus the material that almost certainly recorded the most imitative and faltering steps of a person learning a new skill is missing, and almost certainly for good. Not missing, however, are a few copies of a pamphlet called *Three Stories and Ten Poems* which he published at Dijon in 1923, and we must settle for this. As the title suggests, Hemingway made his debut, a sort of a false start, as a poet. Most of the verse in this volume brings to mind the poetry either of Stephen Crane or of Vachel Lindsay, and is without other real interest. The three stories — "Up in Michigan," "Out of Season," and "My Old Man" — are on the other hand already accomplished performances, and as such were reprinted in *In Our Time*. But they still reveal something of the influences of other writers on this one, and include as well Hemingway's first attempt to work at what has become his major theme.

The clearest direct obligation is to Sherwood Anderson, for "My Old Man" seems transparently Hemingway's version of Anderson's widely reprinted "I Want to Know Why," which had appeared two years earlier. Both stories are about horse racing, told by boys in their own vernacular; in each case the boy has to confront mature problems while undergoing a painful disillusion-ment with an older man he had been strongly attached to. (Hemingway has claimed that he had not read any Anderson when he wrote "My Old Man," but if this is so the coincidences are very remarkable indeed.) "Out of Season," a tale of lovers under the spell of disenchantment, is reminiscent of Scott Fitz-gerald's *The Beautiful and Damned* (1922). But "Up in Michi-gan" is much the most important of the *Three Stories*; it is a tale of initiation, precisely parallel to the stories of Nick Adams soon to be written. It takes place in the locale of "Indian Camp," and just as Nick in that episode was first exposed to violence, brutality, and pain, so in this story a girl named Liz learns a similar lesson, but for girls. The dogged simplicity of "Up in Michigan" suggests both Anderson and Gertrude Stein, but it is too hardheaded for the former, and cut off by its subject matter from the latter. All Hemingway had to do, once he had written it, was to take up a protagonist in whom he could see himself more directly, and he would have the adventures of Nick Adams.

The influence of other writers on even so distinctive a writer as Hemingway is sometimes perceptible even in work that is completely mature. Good cases in point are two of his best and best known stories, "The Snows of Kilimanjaro" and "The Short Happy Life of Francis Macomber." Both are unmistakably Hemingway, and both are substantially dependent on, or allied to, earlier fiction. "The Short Happy Life" is among other things a detailed description of the process of learning the code, and its value. Macomber, a coward, learns the code from Wilson, his professional hunting guide, and becomes in the process, for a short happy lifetime, a man. He confronts danger at first with a terrible fear, and when it comes he bolts and flies in a panic. But on the next occasion he is wakened from a kind of fighting trance to discover that his fear is gone, his manhood attained, and his life (for a moment) begun.

The story is authentic, vintage Hemingway. But insofar as it deals with Macomber's warlike relations with his wife Margot, it is a very close development and intensification of some notions about the relationship of the sexes in America as put down by D. H. Lawrence in an essay he once wrote on Hawthorne's *Scarlet Letter*. And to the much larger extent that it deals with fear and manhood, it is an almost exact reworking of the story Stephen Crane told in *The Red Badge of Courage*, a novel for which Hemingway has expressed his great — possibly excessive — admiration.

Similarly "The Snows of Kilimanjaro" is a story whose technique has been, deservedly, much praised; again few could mistake it for the work of another writer. But two of its basic symbols — of the leopard and the mountain itself — are taken from Dante and Flaubert, and its most unusual structure has an exact precedent in an experimental tale published in 1891 by Ambrose Bierce and called "An Occurrence at Owl Creek Bridge," a story Hemingway is also known to admire. Both stories deal with a man at the point of death who imaginatively experiences

30

his escape in such a realistic fashion that the reader is fooled into believing that it has been made. Both stories open with the situation of impending death, then flash back to explain how the situation came about, and then flash "forward" with the imaginary escape, only to conclude with the objective information that the death has indeed occurred.

Some of Hemingway's longer pieces have similar affiliations. If for instance *To Have and Have Not* does not owe a good deal to such an unlikely combination of books as James Joyce's *Ulysses* and Frank Norris's *Moran of the Lady Letty* (and Jack London's *Sea Wolf*) then we have on our hands a set of impossible coincidences. It is not at all, however, that Hemingway's work seems derived. Gertrude Stein thought it did: "he looks like a modern and he smells of the museums," she said. Edmund Wilson disagreed: "Hemingway should perhaps more than anyone else be allowed to escape the common literary fate of being derived from other people." And Alfred Kazin concurred, writing that he "had no basic relation to any prewar culture."

It seems entirely possible that all of these judgments are wrong. Hemingway has taken a good deal from other writers, but if he smells of the museums Miss Stein's nose was one of the few to detect the odor. Like most writers, he has gone to those who have preceded him for what his experience and taste have made meaningful and attractive to him. With the force of his personality and the skill of his craft he has made what he has borrowed distinctly and undeniably his own.

More striking, however, is the extent to which, once Hemingway got started, other writers began to make it all theirs. There is probably no country in which American books are read whose literature has been entirely unaffected by Hemingway's work; in his own country we are so conditioned to his influence that we hardly ever notice it any more. On the positive side he has taught the values of objectivity and honesty, has helped to purify our writing of sentimentality, literary embellishment, padding, and a superficial artfulness. Almost singlehanded he has revitalized the writing of dialogue. His influence has extended even more pervasively, however, to the realms of the subliterary, and here the results, through no direct fault of his, have been much less appealing. Many writers, of the "tough-detective school" in particular, demonstrate what happens when the attitudes and mannerisms which have meaning in one novelist are taken over by others, for whom they have rather different meanings, or none. Violence is the meaningful core of Hemingway, but the host of novelists and short-story and script writers who have come to trade on him have seized a bag of tricks — usually a mixture of toughness and sex, with protagonists based on crude misunderstandings of one or the other — or both — of the heroes. In their hands the meanings either are cheap and sordid, or have departed altogether.

It is Hemingway's prose style, however, that has been most imitated, and it is as a stylist that he commands the most respect. His prose is easily recognized. For the most part it is colloquial, characterized chiefly by a conscientious simplicity of diction and sentence structure. The words are normally short and common ones and there is a severe economy, and also a curious freshness, in their use. As Ford Madox Ford remarked some time ago, in a line that is often (and justifiably) quoted, the words "strike you, each one, as if they were pebbles fetched fresh from a brook." The typical sentence is a simple declarative one, or a couple of these joined by a conjunction. The effect is of crispness, cleanness, clarity, and a scrupulous care. (And a scrupulous care goes into the composition; Hemingway works very slowly and revises extensively. He claims to have rewritten the last page of *A Farewell to Arms* thirty-nine times, and to have read through the manuscript of *The Old Man and the Sea* some two hundred times before he was finished with it.)

It is a remarkably unintellectual style. Events are described strictly in the sequence in which they occurred; no mind reorders or analyzes them, and perceptions come to the reader unmixed with comment from the author. The impression, therefore, is of intense objectivity; the writer provides nothing but stimuli. Since violence and pain are so often the subject matter, it follows that a characteristic effect is one of irony or understatement. The vision is narrow, and sharply focused.

The dialogue is equally striking, for Hemingway has an ear like a trap for the accents and mannerisms of human speech; this is chiefly why he is able to bring a character swiftly to life. The conversation is far from a simple transcription, however, of the way people talk. Instead the dialogue strips speech to an essential pattern of mannerisms and responses characteristic of the speaker, and gives an illusion of reality that reality itself would not give.

Nothing in this brief account of the "Hemingway style" should seem very surprising, but the purposes, implications, and ultimate meanings of this manner of writing are less well recognized. A style has its own content, and the manner of a distinctive prose style has its own meanings. The things that Hemingway's style most conveys are the very things he says outright. His style is as communicative of the content as the content itself, and is a large and inextricable part of the content. The strictly disciplined controls exerted over the hero and his nervous system are precise parallels to the strictly disciplined sentences. The "mindlessness" of the style is a reflection and expression of the need to "stop thinking" when thought means remembering the things that upset. The intense simplicity of the prose is a means of saying that things must be *made* simple, or the hero is lost, and in "a way you'll never be." The economy and narrow focus of the prose controls the little that can be absolutely mastered. The prose is tense because the atmosphere in which the struggle for control takes place is tense, and the tension in the style expresses that fact.

These notions are scarcely weakened by the reminder that the style was developed and perfected in the same period when the author was reorganizing his personality after the scattering of his forces in Italy. These efforts were two sides of one effort. Hemingway has written, in a story called "Fathers and Sons," that if he wrote some things he could get rid of them; it is equally to the point that he has written them in the style that would get rid of them. The discipline that made the new personality made the prose style that bespoke the personality. The style is the clear voice of the content. It is the end, or aim, of the man, and a goal marvelously won. It is the means of being the man. An old commonplace never had more force than here: the style *is* the man.

One of the most common criticisms of Hemingway used to be that he had wandered too far from his roots, his traditions, and had got lost. People who made this criticism usually said that the author should find a way home to some such tradition as is to be found in a novel like Mark Twain's *Huckleberry Finn* — this one, presumably, because it seems to be by almost unanimous consent the most American of all novels. This is of course the book that Hemingway said all modern American writing comes from; the suspicion is forced on us that someone is confused.

It was the critics who were confused, partly because they missed some of the depths and subtleties in both writers. The curious truth is that if the pattern in Hemingway's work discussed here — the pattern of violence, psychological wounding, escape and death — has any validity, then Hemingway never has got very far from *Huckleberry Finn*. A careful reading of that novel will show precisely that pattern. The *Adventures of Huckleberry Finn* and

34

of Nick Adams are remarkably of a piece. "It made me so sick I most fell out of the tree," says Huck of his exposure to the Grangerford-Shepherdson feud. "I ain't a-going to tell *all* that happened. . . . I wished I hadn't ever come ashore that night to see such things — lots of times I dream about them."

There is so much either hilarious or idyllic in the novel about this boy that we are easily but mistakenly diverted from the spill of blood that gives the book a large part of its meaning and deeply affects Huck. Life on the Mississippi around 1845 could be gory, and Twain based his novel largely on experiences he himself had undergone as a boy, or had known intimately of, and had never quite got over. (We know, for instance, that he witnessed four murders.) A lot of this experience found its way into the book, and it is impossible to understand the novel completely without seeing what all this violence results in. But the results are clear: Huck's overexposure to violence finally wounds him. Each episode makes a mark, and each mark leaves a scar. Every major episode in the novel, with the exceptions only of the rather irrelevant Tom Sawyer scenes at the beginning and conclusion, ends in violence, in physical brutality, and usually in death. All along the way are bloodshed and pain, and there are thirteen separate corpses. The effect of all this, and the only effect that is relevant to the main plot, is that it serves to wound Huck Finn. Either tortured with nightmares or unable to sleep at all ("I couldn't, somehow, for thinking"), he is "made sick" by — among other things — the thought of a man left alone to drown, by the sale of some colored servants, and by the departure of the Duke and the King, tarred, feathered, and astraddle a rail. In addition he is becoming disgusted with mankind in general. Exposed to more bloodshed, drowning, and sudden death than he can handle, he is himself their casualty. And from his own experience Mark Twain could predict: Huck isn't ever going to get over them.

PHILIP YOUNG

Here, transparently, is the pattern of violence and psychological wounding we have been reading in Hemingway. The rest of it, the elements of escape and death, though in part submerged in symbolism, are also demonstrable in the same book. Huck's whole journey is of course made up of a series of escapes — escapes for the most part down a mighty and deeply mysterious river. His strange journey down the glamorous Mississippi, blurred, mythic, and wondrously suggestive, becomes in the end a supremely effortless flight into a dark and silent unknown. Symbolically Huck escapes more than he is aware of, and into something which — if this were literal and not metaphorical — he could not return from. Over and over again his silent, effortless, nighttime departures down the black and mighty stream compel us. In the end they transport us from a noisy, painful, and difficult life to the safety of the last escape of all. In the end as well, Twain is forced to drop Huck and to turn the story over to Tom Sawyer. The reason is not hard to find: Huck had grown too hot to handle. A damaged boy, tortured by the terror he has witnessed and been through, afflicted with insomnia and bad dreams, and voluntarily divorced from the society in which he had grown up, Huck could no longer be managed by a man who had not solved his own complications, many of which he had invested in the boy. What the author did not realize was that in his journey by water he had been hinting at a solution all along: an excessive exposure to violence and death produced first a compulsive fascination with dying, and finally an ideal symbol for it.

The parallel is complete. In both Huck and Nick, Hemingway's generic hero, we have a sensitive, rather passive but courageous and masculine boy, solitary and out of doors, who is dissatisfied with respectability, chiefly as represented by a Bible-quoting woman of the house. Each runs away from home. "Home" in both cases — St. Petersburg or northern Michigan — was a place of violence and pain, but though it was easy to flee the respectability, off on their own both boys came up against brutality harder than ever. Both were hurt by it and both ended by rebelling utterly against a society that sponsored, or permitted, such horror. Nick decides that he is not a patriot, and makes his own peace with the enemy; Huck decides that he will take up wickedness, and go to hell. He lights out for the territory, the hero for foreign lands. Huck and Nick are very nearly twins. Two of our most prominent heroes, Huck and the Hemingway hero, are casualties whom the "knowledge of evil," which Americans are commonly said to lack, has made sick.

This theme of the boy shattered by the world he grows up in is a variation on one of the most ancient of all stories, and one of the greatest of all American stories, which relates the meeting of innocence and experience. It was a primary theme of our first professional man of letters, Charles Brockden Brown, and it has run through our literature ever since. In the latter half of the nineteenth century it was related at what might be called the very poles of our national experience — on the frontier and in Europe — and with the steady flow of travelers abroad it was primarily in Europe that the drama of the meeting of youth and age was enacted. Here developments of the theme ranged all the way from comic and crude accounts of innocents abroad to the subtleties of Hawthorne and James, with their pictures of American visitors under the impact of the European social order.

The story is a great American story not only because it is based on the experience of every man as he grows up, but also on the particular and peculiar history of the country. Once we were fully discovered, established, and unified we began to rediscover the world, and this adventure resulted in our defining ourselves in the light of people who did not seem, to us or to them, quite like us.

The stories of Huck Finn and the Hemingway hero share this general theme, for they tell again what happens when innocence, or a spontaneous virtue, meets with something not at all itself. But they are variations on the theme. The traveling comedians in Europe made spectacles of their ignorance, but usually had the last laugh. The more serious pilgrims were usually enriched at their pain, but showed up well in the process, often displaying a kind of power that comes from purity. But there is nothing subtle about the force that confronts the natural goodness of Huck and Nick. It is violence, an essential experience of the frontier, and also in our time — which is a wartime — of the American in Europe. And there is nothing triumphant about the beating which innocence takes, or about what happens to it after it is beaten.

The repetition of Twain's story by Hemingway establishes a continuity of American experience from one century to another, and reinforces the meaning of either story taken separately. The narrative begins to take on overtones that are larger than the facts themselves would seem to warrant. Indeed we might, conscious that we employ an abused term loosely, call it a "myth." At any rate it is a highly suggestive tale that falls, not surprisingly, within the Christian system and relates once more the fall of man, the loss of paradise. But it is an American myth, and it reveals us in a way that no historical, social, or philosophical treatise can do. It speaks to the people of the country from which it springs, and to the world, if it cares to hear, in such a way as to say: We start out smiling and well disposed to the world and our fellow men. We see ourselves in the image of a naturally good, innocent, and simple boy, eager and expectant. But in the process of our going out into the world we get struck down, somehow, and after that it is hard for us to put ourselves all the way back together again.

This myth seems to bespeak in Americans an innocent desire

for a decent life on the one hand and a sense of betrayal on the other. It says that we would do justly and be kind, that we wished no evil to anyone. But it also says that as we grew up evil was everywhere, and our expectations were sold out. The myth is one attempt to explain us, to ourselves and to the world. It also tries to explain why it is that despite all our other, opposing myths — of success, progress, the certain beneficence of technical advance, and the like — we are neither completely happy nor whole. It says, rather wistfully, we would have been, we could have been, but we were wounded before we were grown by the world we were given to grow in. The original beauty of a new country, the anticipation of the possibilities of life in what seemed the most promising world since Eden, were part of a seduction that went bad and should have ended at the doctor's. This is not a story that we believe literally, of course. No myth is to be taken literally or we would not, nowadays, call it a myth. But in a figurative way, on a metaphorical level, one suspects that we believe something of this sort about our experience in the world.

It remains to say something about Hemingway's world — the world his experience has caused his imagination to create in books. It is, of course, a very limited world that we are exposed to through him. It is, ultimately, a world at war — war either literally as armed and calculated conflict, or figuratively as marked everywhere with violence, potential or present, and a general hostility. The people of this world operate under such conditions — of apprehension, emergency, stiff-lipped fear, and pleasure seized in haste — as are imposed by war. Restricted grimly by the urgencies of war, their pleasures are limited pretty much to those the senses can communicate, and their morality is a harshly pragmatic affair; what's moral is what you feel good after. Related to this is the code, summarizing the virtues of the soldier, the ethic of wartime. The activities of escape go according to the rules of sport, which make up the code of the armistice, the temporary, peacetime modification of the rules of war.

Hemingway's world is one in which things do not grow and bear fruit, but explode, break, decompose, or are eaten away. It is saved from total misery by visions of endurance, competence, and courage, by what happiness the body can give when it is not in pain, by interludes of love that cannot outlast the furlough, by a pleasure in the countries one can visit, or fish and hunt in, and the cafés one can sit in, and by very little else. Hemingway's characters do not "mature" in the ordinary sense, do not become "adult." It is impossible to picture them in a family circle, going to the polls to vote, or making out their income tax returns. It is a very narrow world. It is a world seen through a crack in the wall by a man who is pinned down by gunfire. The vision is obsessed by violence, and insists that we honor a stubborn preoccupation with the profound significance of violence in our time.

We may argue the utter inadequacy of the world Hemingway has refracted and recreated; indeed we should protest against it. It is not the world we wish to live in, and we usually believe that actually we do not live in it. But if we choose to look back over our time, what essential facts can we stack against the facts of violence, evil, and death? We remember countless "minor" wars, and two tremendous ones, and prepare for the day when we may be engaged in a holocaust beyond which we cannot see anything. We may argue against Hemingway's world, but we should not find it easy to prove that it is not the world we have been living in.

It is still too early to know which of all the worlds our writers offer will be the one we shall turn out to have lived in. It all depends on what happens and you never know at the time. "Peace in our time," however, was Hemingway's obscure and ironic prophecy, stated at the start and stuck to. From the beginning his eyes have been focused on what may turn out decades hence to have been the main show. With all his obvious limitations, it is possible that he has been saying many of the truest things of our age truly, and these are materials for the building of a permanent literary reputation.

⤲ Selected Bibliography

Principal Works of Ernest Hemingway

Three Stories and Ten Poems. Paris and Dijon: Contact Publishing Co., 1923.
In Our Time. New York: Boni and Liveright, 1925.
The Torrents of Spring. New York: Scribner's, 1926.
The Sun Also Rises. New York: Scribner's, 1926.
Men without Women. New York: Scribner's, 1927.
A Farewell to Arms. New York: Scribner's, 1929.
Death in the Afternoon. New York: Scribner's, 1932.
Winner Take Nothing. New York: Scribner's, 1933.
Green Hills of Africa. New York: Scribner's, 1935.
To Have and Have Not. New York: Scribner's, 1937.
The Fifth Column and the First Forty-Nine Stories. New York: Scribner's, 1938.
For Whom the Bell Tolls. New York: Scribner's, 1940.
Across the River and into the Trees. New York: Scribner's, 1950.
The Old Man and the Sea. New York: Scribner's, 1952.

Current American Reprints

A Farewell to Arms. New York: Scribner's Text Edition. $1.95.
For Whom the Bell Tolls. New York: Scribner's Text Edition. $2.75.
Hemingway Reader, Charles Poore, ed. New York: Scribner's Text Edition. $2.75.
The Short Stories of Ernest Hemingway. New York: Scribner's Text Edition. $2.75.
The Sun Also Rises. New York: Scribner's Text Edition. $1.45.

Bibliographies

Baker, Carlos. "A Working Checklist of Hemingway's Prose, Poetry, and Journalism — with Notes," *Hemingway: The Writer as Artist.* Princeton, N.J.: Princeton University Press, 1952.
Beebe, Maurice. "Criticism of Ernest Hemingway: A Selected Checklist with an Index to Studies of Separate Works," *Modern Fiction Studies*, 1:36–45 (August 1955).
Samuels, Lee. *A Hemingway Check List.* New York: Scribner's, 1951.

Critical and Biographical Studies

Baker, Carlos. *Hemingway: The Writer as Artist*. Princeton, N.J.: Princeton University Press, 1952.

Fenton, Charles A. *The Apprenticeship of Ernest Hemingway*. New York: Farrar, Straus and Young, 1954.

McCaffery, John K. M., ed. *Ernest Hemingway: The Man and His Work*. Cleveland: World, 1950.

Young, Philip. *Ernest Hemingway*. New York: Rinehart, 1952.

Articles

Beach, Joseph Warren. "How Do You Like It Now, Gentlemen?" *Sewanee Review*, 59:311–28 (Spring 1951).

Bishop, John Peale. "Homage to Hemingway," *New Republic*, 89:39–42 (November 11, 1936).

*————."The Missing All," *Virginia Quarterly Review*, 13:107–21 (Winter 1937).

Cowley, Malcolm. "Hemingway and the Hero," *New Republic*, 101:754–58 (December 4, 1944).

————. "Hemingway at Midnight," *New Republic*, 111:190–95 (August 14, 1944).

*————. "A Portrait of Mister Papa," *Life*, 26:86–101 (January 10, 1949).

Edel, Leon, and Philip Young. "Hemingway and the Nobel Prize" (a debate), *Folio*, 20:18–22 (Spring 1955).

Engstrom, A. G. "Dante, Flaubert and 'The Snows of Kilimanjaro,'" *Modern Language Notes*, 65:203–5 (March 1950).

*Frohock, W. M. "Ernest Hemingway: Violence and Discipline," *Southwest Review*, 32:89–97 and 184–93 (Winter and Spring 1947).

Fussell, Edwin. "Hemingway and Mark Twain," *Accent*, 14:199–206 (Summer 1954).

Gordon, Caroline. "Notes on Hemingway and Kafka," *Sewanee Review*, 57:215–26 (Spring 1949).

*Hemphill, George. "Hemingway and James," *Kenyon Review*, 11:50–60 (Winter 1949).

Hertzel, Leo J. "Hemingway and the Problem of Belief," *Catholic World*, 184:29–33 (October 1956).

*Kashkeen, J. "A Tragedy of Craftsmanship," *International Literature* (U.S.S.R.), no. 5, 1935.

————. "Alive in the Midst of Death," *Soviet Literature*, no. 7, 1956.

---

*All articles preceded by an asterisk are included in McCaffery, *Ernest Hemingway: The Man and His Work*.

Levin, Harry. "Observations on the Style of Hemingway," *Kenyon Review*, 13:581–609 (Autumn 1951).

Lewis, Wyndham. "The Dumb Ox, a Study of Ernest Hemingway," *American Review*, 6:289–312 (June 1934).

Modern Fiction Studies, vol. 1 (August 1955). Essays on Hemingway by Melvin Backman, Tom Burnam, C. Hugh Holman, Bernard S. Oldsey, H. K. Russell, and Green D. Wyrick.

Plimpton, George. "The Art of Fiction XXI. Ernest Hemingway," *Paris Review*,

Ross, Li..*er*, 26:36–62 (May

Savage,..tober 1948).

Schorer,...*n*, William

Van (...1948.

*Schwa...*uthern Review*,

Stein, (...;," *Atlantic Mont

Warren...inter 1947).

——..York: Scribner's

ner's...

West, F...*ch Review*, 4:569

——..*ee Review*, 53:12

*Wilson...e," *Atlantic Mont

UNIVERSITY OF MINNESOTA
PAMPHLETS ON AMERICAN WRITERS

William Van O'Connor, Allen Tate, and
Robert Penn Warren, editors

Willard Thorp, Karl Shapiro, and Philip Rahv, advisers

1. **ERNEST HEMINGWAY** by Philip Young *(published)*.

2. **ROBERT FROST** by Lawrance Thompson *(published)*.

3. **WILLIAM FAULKNER** by William Van O'Connor *(published)*.

HENRY JAMES by Leon Edel *(forthcoming)*.

EUGENE O'NEILL by John Gassner *(forthcoming)*.

MARK TWAIN by Lewis Leary *(forthcoming)*.

UNIVERSITY OF MINNESOTA PRESS, Minneapolis 14
Minnesota, U.S.A.